THE SUN WILL SHINE AGAIN

CYNTHIA GOLDSTEIN MONSOUR

ISBN 9789493418400 (ebook)

ISBN 9789493418394 (paperback)

ISBN 9789493418387 (hardcover)

Publisher: Amsterdam Publishers, The Netherlands

info@amsterdampublishers.com

The Sun Will Shine Again is part of the series Holocaust Books for Young Adults

Copyright © Cynthia Goldstein Monsour 2025

Cover art by Harriet Sobie Goldstein. Entitled, "Hope," this silkscreen depicts the canal in Anderlecht, a municipality of Brussels, Belgium, where Bruno and his twin brother, Jack, searched for coal.

All Rights Reserved. No part of this publication may be reproduced or transmitted in any form or by any means, electronic or mechanical, including photocopy, recording or any other information storage and retrieval system, without prior permission in writing from the publisher.

CONTENTS

Prologue	1
Age Three	3
Age Four	7
Age Five	9
Age Six	14
Age Seven	17
Age Eight	20
Age Nine	23
Epilogue	31
Photos	35
Guide for Adults and Teachers	43
About the Author	49
Amsterdam Publishers Holocaust Library	51

For my father, Bruno

and my daughter, Tess

PROLOGUE

When you're living through historical events, you don't necessarily realize it. That's especially so when you're a child. That was the case for my grandpa.

My name is Tess and I am ten years old. By the time my grandpa was my age, he had survived World War II.

He knew the sadness and pain of being separated from his mother and father, of not knowing if he would ever see them again, of being alone in an apartment building where everyone else had been taken by bad men, of being hungry and cold and not knowing if things would ever get better.

To me, these are just stories, but to my grandpa, they are memories of a dark time.

Through the darkness, he found light with his twin brother by his side.

These are his memories.

This is his story.

AGE THREE

On my third birthday, my country, Austria, was taken over by a bigger, neighboring country called Germany. Germany was led by a man named Adolf Hitler, who was part of the Nazi political party.

Hitler blamed the Jews and anyone who thought differently for any problems in Germany. He told horrible lies and people believed him. He spoke in loud, angry tones to rouse hate and violence. Under Adolf Hitler, Germany became known as Nazi Germany.

I remember my third birthday celebration in my grandparents' apartment in Vienna, the capital city of Austria. From their balcony, I was able to watch the Nazi soldiers marching in the street below.

The crowds of people in the street were excited and happy. They were shouting, "*Heil Hitler*" in German, which means "Hail Hitler," and "*Sieg Heil*," which means "Hail victory," over and over again. The year was 1938.

I became excited too by watching the cheering crowd. I put my hand to my head in the same way that the people below me in the street were doing and I said, "Heil Hitler!"

I was immediately told that a Jewish boy does not say that. I felt ashamed. It was my third birthday and suddenly, life was changing. This is when I learned that being Jewish made us different.

My third birthday was actually a significant day in Austrian history. The date is known as the *Anschluss* in German, which is the official unification of the nation of Austria with Nazi Germany.

After the Anschluss, normal life in Austria became impossible for Jews. The Nazis created anti-Jewish laws. Jews were forced to give up their businesses and their homes. Jewish children had to stop going to school.

My parents had a difficult decision to make: should we leave Austria? They didn't want to leave their own parents, who were hesitant to start their lives over in a new country. And on the other hand, leaving Austria was not easy because many countries, such as the United States of America, were not allowing Jews to enter.

The decision was made for them, however, on the night of November 9, 1938. The Nazis' police, called the Gestapo, knocked loudly on our apartment door. They arrested my father. My twin brother, mother, and I were crying as they took him away. We couldn't believe what was happening and we felt powerless.

The Gestapo brought him outside to the street, where they had gathered many Jewish men. In the middle of the chaos, the leader of the group took him around the corner of our building. And he told him that as the father of beautiful twin boys, he should disappear quickly. Then my father was unexpectedly let go.

This night is known as *Kristallnacht* in German, which means "Crystal Night" in English. The name refers to the broken glass left in the streets after the destruction of Jewish businesses, homes, and synagogues.

It was a night of violence and brutality against Jews and my father was lucky to have been released. Many fathers were not as lucky. Kristallnacht made it clear to my parents that staying in Austria was no longer an option.

AGE FOUR

When I was four years old, we left behind nearly everything that we owned and we arrived in Brussels, the capital city of Belgium, a country in northwest Europe. We moved into a small apartment in a section of Brussels, where other Jewish refugees like us had settled.

A refugee is a person seeking safety in a new country after leaving their homeland due to war or danger.

I don't remember a lot about this time, but I know that Jews arriving from Austria and Germany were not trusted by the Belgians.

We didn't speak either French or Flemish, which were the two official languages spoken in Belgium. And my parents were required to register with the police department as "*Étrangers,*" which is the French word for foreigners.

My brother and I did not have any toys with us in Belgium. We still had our imaginations though and we played inside of the apartment. We would take a chair and pretend that it was a car. We did our best to keep busy.

AGE FIVE

I was five years old when Nazi Germany invaded Belgium in May of 1940. When this happened, all foreigners in Belgium, particularly Germans and Austrians, were considered the enemy. This included German-speaking Jewish refugees like us.

Since my parents were registered as "Étrangers," my father was arrested by the Belgian police along with other German-speaking Jewish men. My father was ordered to appear at a government building in the center of Brussels. We went with him.

He was instructed to board a bus once we got there. I remember that he had a small suitcase. We hoped that he would only be held for a brief time. But this isn't what happened. My father along with the other men were deported from Belgium to an internment camp in southern France, called Saint-Cyprien. There was no intention to bring them back soon, if at all.

An internment camp is where groups of people are held as prisoners without charges, usually during wartime.

The Saint-Cyprien camp was a terrible place. It was overcrowded and there was hardly any food or water. From there, my father was transferred to a second internment camp, named Gurs, which was equally awful.

Fortunately, my father had a small French-to-German dictionary with him. The dictionary was meant to help him understand French. But in Gurs, it helped him to survive. He was able to trade pages from it with other prisoners in exchange for food, such as a small piece of bread. The other prisoners used the pages for toilet paper.

My mother was now on her own in a new country with two young boys. We felt scared and uncertain about the future. Everything was new to us – the language, the city, the culture, the people. Our father was gone. We didn't know where he was, or even if he was alive.

One day, as a small treat to cheer us up, my mother took us for a soda in the café on the street level of our small apartment building. The three of us were chatting in German, enjoying our cold sodas on a hot day. I felt happy. Suddenly though, we noticed that a stern looking man sitting at a nearby table was watching us. We grew tense when he began to walk over. I was afraid that he would take my mother away. Instead, he spoke to her for a while in German. Although the man did not seem particularly friendly, towards the end of their conversation I heard him say in German: "*Eines Tages wird die Sonne wieder auf dich und deine Familie scheinen.*" In English, this means: "One day, the sun will shine on you and your family again." This hopeful comment has stayed with me to this day.

A few days later, we were at home in the afternoon when there was an unexpected knock at the front door. We were always nervous when someone was at the door. But this time, it was a complete shock to see my mother's beloved older sister, Fani. It was a wonderful surprise for us. My brother and I called her *"Tante,"* which means Aunt in French.

Tante Fani had entered Belgium illegally from Austria. This meant that she didn't have an identity card showing her photograph and personal information, such as her name and birthdate. The Nazis frequently requested to see a person's identity card. It was dangerous to be without one because it meant that you could be arrested at any time.

Daily life in Brussels was becoming increasingly uncertain and in June of 1940, many people packed up their belongings. The British were evacuating soldiers by boat from Belgium to England across the North Sea. There were rumors that the British would evacuate women and children too.

An evacuation occurs when people are moved from an area in danger to a safer location.

We packed our bags. My mother and Tante Fani paid a truck driver to take the four of us north towards the coast. We sat in the back of the truck with many other desperate people and their belongings.

However, at some point during the journey, the driver discovered that Tante Fani did not have an identity card. Once he learned this, he refused to take her further. We couldn't leave without her, so we all got out of the truck.

We found ourselves on the side of the road with hundreds of people walking north to the coast.

After a while, we learned from the people walking in the opposite direction that the boats to England were only taking soldiers, not women and children. We had come such a long way, only to turn around and head back. It was a sad and confusing realization.

We walked for a long time. I saw horrifying things, such as dead cows and horses; and worse, I saw dead people. I was tired. I felt that I couldn't walk any longer. I remember telling my mother that I just wanted to die. But we kept going, putting one foot in front of the other. Eventually, my mother found us a ride in a different truck and we made it back to our small apartment in Brussels.

AGE SIX

My mother took in sewing work to help us survive. She could do the work from our apartment, where we all spent most of our time.

I remember sitting with my brother while my mother was sewing when an unfamiliar man with a brown beard arrived at our front door. It was August of 1941. I didn't recognize this man at all. But when my mother saw him, she cried out in happiness. He was dirty and he looked different to me, but once he spoke, I recognized his voice. It was my father! He had been gone for more than a year.

He had escaped from Camp des Milles, his third internment camp, where he had been transferred from Gurs. Like the previous camps, Camp de Milles was in southern France. In order to reach us in Belgium, my father had been on a long and risky journey through Nazi-occupied France.

He told us that he travelled with another man, who escaped at the same time as him. I don't know any details about this man, but I'm grateful that my father had a companion for the dangerous journey.

We moved into a new apartment soon after my father returned. My parents felt that it would be best to change our location because the Gestapo was actively searching for Jews.

My father found work in a factory making fur-lined clothing used by the Nazi soldiers fighting on the Russian front. While there was no pay for this work, he received special papers for his family.

My parents hoped that the papers might provide us with some protection. The factory provided the special papers because it did not want to lose its free labor, who were aiding the German war effort.

In September, my brother and I started our first year of public school. It was dangerous for us to be outside of our apartment, but I was excited to learn and to be around other children. Plus, my brother and I were in the same class.

But the routine and excitement of attending school was short lived. By December, Jewish children were forbidden to attend public schools in Belgium.

AGE SEVEN

When my brother and I were seven-years-old, we spent much of our time inside of the apartment. There was no more school to escape to. It was a time of danger and we lived day by day. Jews could now be arrested at any time for any arbitrary reason.

Each day, my parents tried to evade arrest to keep us alive a little longer. My parents were also deeply concerned for their own parents – my grandparents. In Vienna, my grandparents on my father's side were arrested and deported to a ghetto in a small town in Poland.

Ghettos are places where Jews were segregated and forced to live by the Nazis.

The Nazis used the ghettos to separate, humiliate, and control Jews. Life inside the ghetto was hard. They were overcrowded and Jews were not allowed to work. It was hard to put food on the table without money.

My grandparents on my mother's side were arrested in Vienna as well. They were deported to a different ghetto in Poland along with one of my uncles, named Moritz, and his wife and children.

My parents sent letters and packages to both of their parents and Uncle Moritz. The letters were meant to lift their spirits with updates on me and my brother.

My mother also sent special packages to Uncle Moritz. They were clever. She would send him one shoe without the other. Why do you think she would do that? Well, the Nazis frequently opened up packages sent to Jews in the ghettos. They took anything of value. But who would want one shoe?

My mother would then send a second package to Uncle Moritz containing the missing shoe. He could exchange it for something they needed like food.

The pressure on Jews was increasing. It was May of 1942 when a new law required all Jews in Belgium over age six to wear a small yellow star on their outer clothing. The yellow star was yet another way of separating and humiliating Jews. Wearing the yellow star also made it easier for the Nazis to identify who to harass and arrest.

My parents and Tante Fani sewed the star to the front of their coats. The star was made of yellow cloth and it had the letter "J" on it in black ink. The "J" stood for "*Juif,*" which means Jew in French.

Though we were now seven, my parents did not want us to wear the yellow star. They decided that it was safer to have us move around Brussels without standing out as Jewish.

AGE EIGHT

Food was scarce and I was hungry all of the time. But sometimes, Tante Fani had a little extra money for a small treat. One day, she gave me enough coins to buy a single egg at the local store close to our apartment. Eggs were rare and expensive. It was a special occasion to have one.

I was excited! I ran the entire way to the store. The egg was brown and I held it carefully in my hands. I had a feeling that Tante Fani was going to use it to cook something delicious.

Walking quickly home, I passed through a tunnel that ran underneath the overhead train line. And that is where it happened – I dropped the egg. I remember standing in silence, watching the yellow and the white running out on the pavement. I even thought about trying to put the egg back into its shell, but I knew that was impossible.

I was afraid to go home. Everyone would be disappointed in me for being so careless. I stayed in the tunnel alone for a long time. Eventually, my brother was sent to look for me. I had been crying and when he found me and saw the broken egg, he began to cry too.

But my brother convinced me to go home. When we got there, my parents and Tante Fani were so relieved to see us, they didn't care at all about the egg. They had feared that the Gestapo had taken me.

Winters in Brussels were cold and damp. Our apartment was close to a canal, where boats would unload coal with big cranes onto waiting trucks. Coal was a luxury. We could use it to heat the little stove in our apartment.

My brother and I would sometimes wait with other children as the coal was being unloaded hoping that a few pieces would fall out. Once the scraps of coal hit the ground, the children would push and shove one another to grab the fallen pieces. We got lucky sometimes and snatched a few ourselves.

I remember one day that I was not so fortunate, though. It was particularly cold and damp, which was good motivation to find pieces of coal.

I was having some success until a group of older boys noticed. They grabbed me and threw me into a hole, taking all of my coal! The hole was too deep for me to climb out of. Once the older boys left, my brother helped me out. After that day, I'm not sure if we ever went back again to look for coal.

AGE NINE

Right around our ninth birthday in March of 1944, my brother and I were alone in our apartment when we heard loud police sirens. Yelling, shouting, and loud stomping of the heavy boots of the Gestapo followed.

Our building had four stories and we lived on the top floor. We could hear the Gestapo pounding on the apartment doors below us, and their movement up the stairs. Soon, there came the loud knocks on our own door.

My brother and I were terrified, but we had no choice but to open the door. As soon as we did, two men ordered us to pack a few clothes and go with them. Tears streamed down my face.

I thought that this was the end and we were going to be killed. But my brother thought quickly and he began to speak in German to the Gestapo. He said that we had special papers. Then he went to the little stove, where we kept the papers safe. These were the same papers that said that our father worked in a factory, making fur-lined clothing for the Nazis fighting on the Russian front. My brother handed them to the Gestapo.

We watched and waited in fear as the men disagreed loudly about whether to take us or not. Finally, we heard the leader of the group say firmly: *"Nein! Die Kinder bleiben hier."* In English, this means: "No! The children stay."

After the Gestapo left our apartment, my brother and I were in shock. The building was empty except for us. Everyone else had been taken. It was suddenly very quiet. We waited anxiously for our parents to come home, fearing that at any moment, the Gestapo would come back for us.

That same evening, my parents moved us into a new small apartment. It was too dangerous to stay in our current one. The Gestapo could return in the middle of the night to take us all. My father borrowed a wooden pushcart from a friend, and we put all of our belongings in it.

After about a mile walk, we reached our new home. It was one large room and like the previous apartments, there was no kitchen and no running water. But I remember that it had a nice little balcony that looked out to the house across the street and a small green park.

This narrow escape weighed on my parents. It was getting more dangerous to continue to hide us in plain sight. My mother learned about a Benedictine monk from Belgium who was hiding Jewish children in Catholic orphanages, Catholic boarding schools, on farms with families, and even with his own family members. His name was Père Bruno Reynders. "*Père*" means father in French and it is also the title used for a priest.

Hiding Jewish children was dangerous. It was a form of resistance, a way of standing up to the Nazis. Making contact with Père Bruno needed to be done carefully and secretly. Somehow, my parents were able to get in touch with him and arrangements were made for me and my brother to go into hiding.

In preparation for meeting with Père Bruno, my mother sewed backpacks for us from an old bed sheet, which she dyed brown. We packed a small amount of clothing in them. Then, the three of us met Père Bruno at the *Gare du Nord* in Brussels – which is the North Train Station.

On the train platform, my mother walked us over to Père Bruno. She greeted him calmly and then, just as quickly, she left. My brother and I were warned not to hug or kiss her good-bye because that might attract attention.

Père Bruno was dressed in regular clothes, rather than the traditional tunic of a Benedictine monk. His acts of resistance and opposition to Nazi Germany had put him in the crosshairs of the Nazis and they were searching for him. He needed to blend in.

Though Père Bruno was a stranger to me and I was nervous to leave my parents, he made me feel safe. He was a calm and gentle man. On the train, we had to be well-behaved and quiet boys. This was difficult for me because I was excited to be on the train!

Père Bruno brought us to the home of a kind doctor, and he left us there to spend the night. The doctor's house was beautiful with a big circular driveway. My brother and I ate well and we even rode bicycles for the first time in our lives. We found them lying in the driveway and we decided to try them.

The next morning, we traveled by car with the doctor, where we were disguised as two sick boys, covered with blankets in the backseat. Along the way, our car was stopped by Nazi soldiers. The doctor told them that we were sick and in need of medical attention. We even coughed to help convince the soldiers.

We eventually arrived at our final destination. It was a Catholic orphanage, located in a village called Maaseik, which is near the Belgian border with another country – Holland. It was April of 1944.

My brother and I had to assume a new last name and memorize a new life story. We were now in hiding pretending to be Christian boys. We were allowed to keep our own first names, thankfully, because it would have been confusing for us to remember new ones.

There were around thirty boys in the orphanage. We went to church every morning, learning Catholic prayers. I tried to blend in and kept my Jewish identity hidden. But I always remembered who I was. I thought of my parents a lot and I prayed that I would get to see them again one day.

I felt safe in the orphanage, though. Going to church and school was a relief for me after being in hiding in our apartment in Brussels. The food wasn't great, but it was better than being hungry.

Each day, all of the children would walk to the church in a line from the orphanage. I was in the line one day when a woman came up to me and gave me a pair of woolen shorts. The woman must have noticed the big hole in mine, which I wore every day. Her kindness meant a lot to me. I've never forgotten it.

By August of 1944, there were signs that Nazi Germany was losing the war. The Allied forces, which included the armies of the United States, Great Britain, Canada, and the Soviet Union, were advancing through France. And at the end of August, France was liberated by the Allied soldiers.

Liberation meant the retreat of the Germans and the end of occupation by Nazi Germany.

Though the Germans were still occupying Belgium, my parents decided that they needed to be with us if Belgium was liberated too. Somehow they learned where we were hidden. I'm not sure how they found out since the location of the children hidden by Père Bruno was a secret. If the Nazis learned of the location of even one hidden child, it could put every hidden child and rescuer at risk.

My mother boarded a train from Brussels and embarked on a dangerous journey to find us. Eventually, her train couldn't continue because the railway tracks were bombed out. She exited the train and found herself in an unfamiliar village.

At the village's train station, my mother noticed that a Gestapo agent started to follow her. She darted into a nearby church to get away. There were a lot of people inside seeking shelter and protection. The Gestapo agent didn't follow her and she spent the night there.

The next morning, before leaving the church, my mother turned her wool coat inside out, so that it was a different color. She tried to look like a different person in case the Gestapo agent was waiting outside. Thankfully, he wasn't there and she continued on her way.

I remember when I first saw my mother, I thought I was dreaming. While in the orphanage, I worried constantly that I might never see my parents again and now, here my mother was in front of me. We hugged for a long time. Then we packed up our belongings and the three of us left the orphanage together. And, somehow, I can't remember how, we made our way back to our apartment in Brussels.

In Brussels, the war was changing quickly and hope was in the air. It was September of 1944 when Belgium was liberated by the Allies. People poured into the streets of Brussels to celebrate the end of the Nazi regime. The grown-ups went wild. They were dancing and singing with joy. There was a lot of shouting of *"Vive la Liberté,"* in French, which means "Long Live Liberty!"

Some people broke into the storage facilities, where the Nazis had kept their food supplies. They took all of the remaining food. The Nazis had eaten well during the war while the rest of us starved.

The Allies, mainly young British, Canadian, and American soldiers, drove through the streets of Brussels in their jeeps, trucks, and tanks. There was so much happiness and noise!

I remember the soldiers throwing chewing gum and chocolates to me and my brother as we chased after their vehicles in a pack of children. It had been a long time since I tasted chocolate.

I will never forget that moment in the sunlight, and the taste of the sweet chocolate. It felt like a dream, but it wasn't. It was real.

EPILOGUE

On May 8, 1945, when my grandpa was ten years old, the same age that I am now, World War II officially ended in Europe.

This day is known as Victory in Europe Day or V-E Day. It marks the unconditional surrender of Nazi Germany to the Allied forces and it's celebrated as a national holiday in many European countries.

Seven years of my grandpa's childhood were spent under Nazi oppression. By the time that World War II was over, six million European Jews had been murdered. And more than one million five hundred thousand of them were children. The systematic murder of the Jewish people by the Nazis is known as the Holocaust.

In Belgium, Père Bruno Reynders led an extensive underground rescue effort that saved the lives of more than three hundred Jewish children, including my grandpa and his brother. He took countless risks in order to save as many children as possible. Without Père Bruno's heroism, certainly many more innocent children would have been murdered.

In 1964, he was recognized as one of the Righteous Among the Nations. This is a title given by Israel to non-Jews who risked their own lives in order to save Jews during World War II.

Many members of my grandpa's family were killed in the Holocaust, including ones mentioned in this story – all four of my grandpa's grandparents, Uncle Moritz, his wife, and children.

My grandpa's parents kept the letters that they received from their own parents and Uncle Moritz written from the ghettos in Poland. These letters show hope that one day they would all be together again. They are first-hand narratives of the Nazi persecution of the Jews. And my family decided to donate them to the United States Holocaust Museum in Washington, D.C.

Today, you can visit the three internment camps where my grandpa's father was held. Saint-Cyprien and Gurs are memorial sites. Camp de Milles is one as well, but it is also a history museum. It is the only large internment camp still intact in France.

My grandpa and his family never returned to live in Austria. There was too much trauma and loss to do that. Instead, they tried to rebuild their lives in Brussels.

Tante Fani opened a second-hand clothing shop. And each Sunday, she would sell her goods at a flea market in the center of Brussels. My grandpa and his brother had the job of making sure people did not steal anything. My grandpa once had to run after a man who tried to take a jacket after trying it on!

When my grandpa and his brother turned thirteen-years-old, they celebrated their Bar Mitzvah. A Bar Mitzvah is an important coming-of-age ritual in Judaism. This was the first big family gathering since my grandpa's third birthday in Austria. Surviving family members traveled to Belgium from other countries, like the United Kingdom and France, to be there.

As time went on, my grandpa's parents felt that there would be more opportunities for their sons in the United States of America. My grandpa was fourteen-years-old when he boarded a ship in Le Havre, France with his parents and brother. They crossed the Atlantic Ocean and settled in New York City. They had to learn yet another new language – English. My grandpa and his brother were thrown right into American culture and began high school in Queens. They were given the nicknames, "Frenchie number one" and "Frenchie number two." My grandpa can't remember if he was number one or two!

Both my grandpa and his brother graduated university and led successful careers as civil engineers. They both married, became fathers and eventually, grandfathers. They remain best friends to this day, speaking every evening by phone.

My grandpa's mother saved the yellow star that she was forced to wear during World War II. My grandpa has it now. I have held it in my hands. It is very small and faded. But I know that this small piece of old cloth holds a powerful story.

And it is a part of my story.

PHOTOS

Babies in Vienna, Austria. My grandpa's twin brother, Jack, my grandpa's mother, and my grandpa, Bruno.

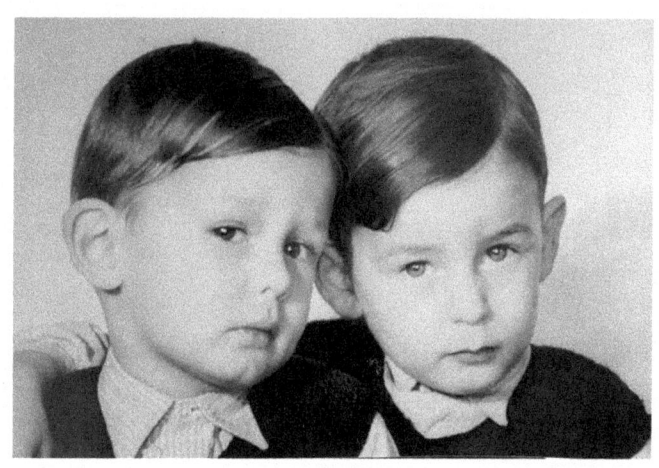

Age 3 in Vienna, Austria. My grandpa's twin brother, Jack and my grandpa, Bruno.

Age 6 in Brussels, Belgium. My grandpa's brother, Jack, my grandpa's mother, and my grandpa, Bruno.

Age 9 in Brussels, Belgium. My grandpa, Bruno, my grandpa's father, and my grandpa's brother, Jack. My grandpa's father is holding his briefcase high to cover the yellow star on his suit jacket.

Age 9 at the Kolonie Saint Jan Berchmans in Maaseik, Belgium while in hiding. My grandpa, Bruno, is kneeling in the second row, second from right. My grandpa's brother, Jack, is standing directly behind him.

Age 11 in Brussels, Belgium. My grandpa's father, my grandpa's brother, Jack, my grandpa, Bruno, and my grandpa's mother.

Age 13 in Brussels, Belgium. My grandpa, Bruno, and his brother, Jack, at their Bar Mitzvah.

This is me, Tess, on the Jewish holiday of Passover with my grandpa.

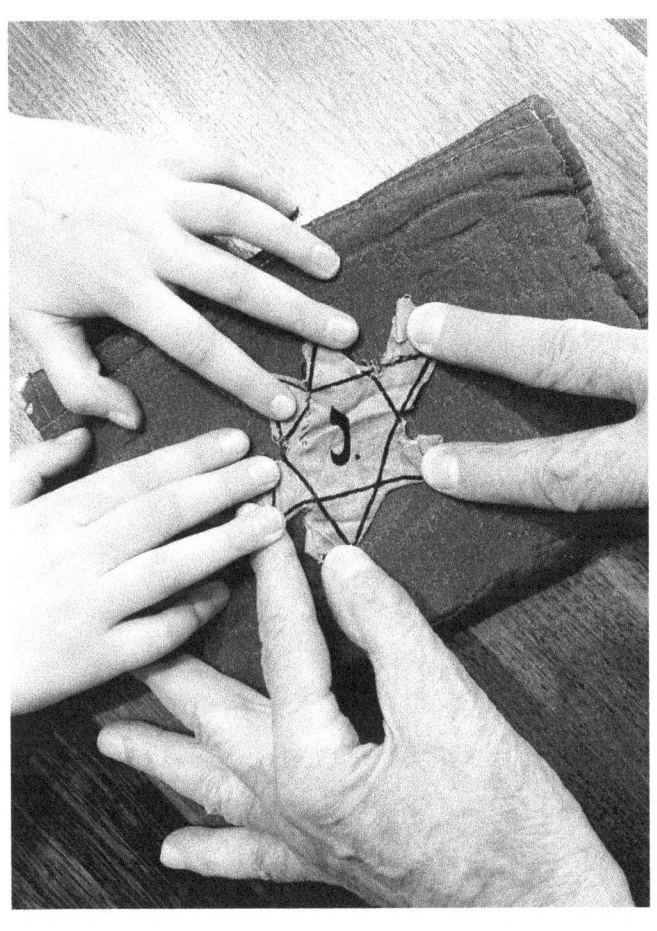

My grandpa and I, holding the yellow star that
belonged to my grandpa's mother.

GUIDE FOR ADULTS AND TEACHERS

For children interested in understanding what it was like to be a child during the Holocaust, like Bruno, these activities might be helpful:

1. Understanding your own family history

Tessa was curious about her grandfather's childhood.

- What are you curious about?
- Think of questions to ask an older relative.

2. The theme of bravery

Bruno and his family exhibited fortitude and bravery as they tried to stay ahead of danger.

• What events in the book showed the family's bravery?

• What qualities do you think make someone brave?

• Has there been a time in your life when you needed to be brave?

3. The connection between the brothers

Bruno and his twin brother were one another's constant companion. They supported each other and provided friendship during a difficult period of their lives.

• How did their strong bond help them to survive?

• Thinking about your own family and close friends, in what ways are you helpful to them?

4. Bruno learned four languages during his childhood

German was Bruno's native language. In order to adapt to new countries, he learned French, Flemish, and English.

• What language(s) does your family speak at home?

• If you could learn a new language, what would it be?

5. Your sense of self

Bruno and his twin brother had to assume new identities when they were hidden by Père Bruno. They had to remember new last names and they could not share their Jewish religion.

• What are the characteristics that define you?

• How would you feel having to pretend to be someone else?

6. The theme of resilience

Being able to handle difficult times helped Bruno and his family survive the Holocaust.

• In what ways did the family adapt to hardship?

• Think of a challenge that you've encountered in your life. How did you grow from this experience?

• Bruno's family never gave up hope for the future. Draw a picture of what you imagine your life will be like in the future.

ABOUT THE AUTHOR

Cynthia Goldstein Monsour studied political science at Barnard College, Columbia University focusing on refugees and human rights. During college, she also studied abroad in Aix-en-Provence, France not far from where her grandfather was interned during World War II. She continued on to law school to pursue her interests in conflict resolution and writing. She currently lives in New Jersey with her husband, daughter, and two cats.

The inspiration for this book came one day while watching her father and then six-year-old daughter having fun playing a card game. Their connection made clear the responsibility of passing on her father's story of survival to her daughter and future generations.

AMSTERDAM PUBLISHERS HOLOCAUST LIBRARY

The series **Holocaust Books for Young Adults** consists of the following novels, based on true stories:

The Boy behind the Door. How Salomon Kool Escaped the Nazis. Inspired by a True Story, by David Tabatsky

Running for Shelter. A True Story, by Suzette Sheft

The Precious Few. An Inspirational Saga of Courage based on True Stories, by David Twain with Art Twain

Dark Shadows Hover, by Jordan Steven Sher

The Sun will Shine Again, by Cynthia Goldstein Monsour

www.ingramcontent.com/pod-product-compliance
Lightning Source LLC
LaVergne TN
LVHW061536070526
838199LV00028B/604/J